LET A NEW EARTH RISE

LET A NEW EARTH RISE

RIO GRANDE VALLEY
YOUTH ANTHOLOGY

—

EDITED BY MCALLEN POET LAUREATES:
Edward Vidaurre, Rodney Gomez,
and Priscilla Celina Suarez

Copyright © 2019
by **FlowerSong Books**
in McAllen, Texas.
www.flowersongbooks.com

ISBN 13: 978-1-7338092-8-3

Published in the United States of America.
First Edition.

No part of this book may be reproduced without written permission from the publisher.

All inquiries and permission requests should be addressed to the Publisher.

Preface

As a child, I had the kind of parents who told me I could be anything I wanted to be --the sky was the limit, and so they encouraged me to dream big. It was their constant love and support that helped me gain the confidence in myself to be who I am today. Because of them and their unwavering love, I have never been afraid to try, never been afraid to fail, and have never been afraid to succeed.

My story is a fortunate one; and although I feel every child in the world should have that kind of support, unfortunately, many of them do not. As a former ELA teacher in a low-social economic area, I witnessed first-hand the daily struggles most children faced in our community. For many of them, school was a safe haven. Many of my students came to school to take refuge from the blazing, unmerciful Texas heat and it gave them a place to stay warm when the weather dropped drastically to extremely low temperatures. It was also a place for them to get at least two meals a day without judgment. I saw that these kids were dreamers, just as I was when I was their age. Although our backgrounds were different, we spoke and dreamed in the same language. I saw that they loved to read fiction to escape the harsh realities of life, and many of these kids were writers with stories so pure, so raw, and so real that I was humbled they trusted me with their words. They acknowledged in themselves that just because they encountered difficulties in life, it did not mean they could not have dreams. As a matter of fact, it was those difficulties that drove them to dream bigger.

I sincerely believe only the courageous write. And we have some of the most courageous poets with words bursting at the seams, needing a positive outlet, yearning for release here in our community. The Rio Grande Valley is bursting with talent. Our young people have something to say and their voices are something we need to listen to.

To be a poet is to be extraordinary. They possess a noble

gift; they are able to see the world differently, and they have the ability to paint pictures with words. I am so grateful that our youth - these dreamers - have advocates such as Edward Vidaurre, Rodney Gomez, and Priscilla Celina Suarez to believe in them. Who give them these wonderful opportunities to become published poets.

I am thankful for the teachers and librarians who encourage and cultivate these young minds to write and express themselves through poetry. WE are extremely fortunate to see the fruit of their labor in this anthology. There is so much heart poured into these pages, so much soul unleashed in black and white, and it is an honor to read their hopes and dreams. May they continue to keep dreaming, may they continue to keep writing and may we all take the time to advocate for the arts in our community - and most importantly, be an advocate for our young people in the RGV.

Si vas a soñar, sueña en grande.

■ *Margie Longoria*
   YA Librarian
   Founder of Border Book Bash: Celebrating Teens and Tweens of the RGV

Contents

I. Light

Music in Me | Danielle Garcia 2

La Luz Está Llegando | Alexa Aguilar 3

Rain Clouds | Elvira S. Castillo 4

Moon | Ananda Nandigam 5

Light | Eyden Gonzalez 7

La Llama | Cesia Hernández 9

Post-Breakup | Samuel David Alonso Jr. 11

La Flor | Luis Enrique Garza 12

Una Vez Mas | Sofia Elizondo 13

Once Again | Sofia Elizondo 14

S.O.S. | Lizbeth Leal 15

Feliz | Saraí López 16

Tempting Fire | Juliana Perez 18

II. Flight

The Weight | Elvira S. Castillo 20

Same Old Lies | Elvira S. Castillo 22

Wings | Lizbeth Leal 24

Renacida | Fabiola Chávez 25

Rebirth | Fabiola Chávez 26

The Liar | Samuel David Alonso Jr. 27

Bartend Her | Krista A. Olivarez 28

The Cloud | Ananda Nandigam 30

Phoenix | Eyden Gonzalez 32

Bloom | Krista A. Olivarez 34

Renacimiento | Grecia A. Elizondo 35

III. Growth

Teen Mind | Lizbeth Leal 37

Renacimiento | Isaura Castillo 38

Modernización | Ángel Guerra 39

Renovación | Karina Montoya 40

Difficult Renovation | Omar Venegas 41

Renovación Difícil | Omar Venegas 42

Thinking Like Flowers | Kayla De León 43

Pensando Como Las Flores | Kayla De León 45

Forbidden Fruit | Samuel David Alonso Jr. 47

Vampire Teeth | Samuel David Alonso Jr. 48

Mother and Man | Andrew Van Wagoner 50

One More Day | Joel A. Sanchez 52

Puzzle | Eyden Gonzalez 54

Mary | Eyden Gonzalez 55

Between the Lines | Joran Cuanang 57

Vision | Vanessa Vega 60

IV. Glimpses

Not in My Dream | Samuel David Alonso Jr. 63

Hanging Out on the Threshold | Krista A. Olivarez 65

The Attic | Krista A. Olivarez 66

The Early Worm | Andrew Van Wagoner 67

Love | Yadira Rocha 68

My Guy | Kendra Cornjeo 69

It's Not | Kendra Cornjeo 70

People | Kendra Cornjeo 71

Why? | Kendra Cornjeo 72

Problems | Juliana Perez 73

The Stray | Juliana Perez 75

Flash Back | Juliana Perez 77

Phoenix | Jada T.R. Cantu-Cabrera 78

V. Rise

Rise | Nohelí Alejandra González 81

Through the Concrete | Diego Flores 82

A través del concreto | Diego Flores 83

The Calm before the Storm | Miranda Aguayo........... 84

La Calma Antes de la Tormenta | Miranda Aguayo 85

Renacimiento: El sonido | Saraí López 86

Renacimiento: Volver a nacer | Amanda Chapa 87

Renacimiento para redención | Érick Gonzáles 88

Renaissance for Redemption | Érick Gonzáles 89

Erroneous Perception | Dibany M. Guerra 90

School Snooze | Danaii Elizondo 92

Survival of the Fittest | Juliana Perez 94

Healing | Eyden Gonzalez 96

Overcome | Sujeis Perez..97

Our Art of Rebirth | Vanessa Vega..........................99

About the Editors..101

I. Light

"I meet you with my heart in my hand."
-Gloria E. Anzaldúa

MUSIC IN ME

Music is everywhere
In the air we breathe, in the food we eat
Music is like skin
Attached to the body
Protects, defines, identifies
Shields one from pain
Individualizes one from another
Connects one to our future self
Reconnects one to our past self
A connection so strong, it brings a feeling of self-belonging
Beauty is within lyrics that amplify our brains
Sounds that ignite with passion
Used as an escape
To feel free
Like a bird during migration season
Winter, summer, fall
Unique yet full of beauty
Guitars, drums, pianos
Different, yet graceful
Sounds so powerful
Notes engraved in my heart

Danielle Garcia
12th Grade
Sharyland High School
McAllen, TX

LA LUZ ESTÁ LLEGANDO

Aquí no brilla la luz del sol.
Repleta de temor estoy
luz y calma tengo que encontrar
tan oscuro que hasta la luz del sol no se ve.

Atrapada en una tormenta me encuentro yo
ahogándome en mi temor...
¿Habrá una manera de escapar de esto?

De lejos miro algo brillar,
Una luz está por llegar
sólo hay que esperar...

La luz está llegando
el temor poco a poco se evapora y se convierte en confianza
me he renovado y tranquila estoy
no hay nada a que temer

todo mi temor desapareció

la luz al fin llegó.

Alexa Aguilar
10th Grade
La Joya Early College High School
Sullivan City, TX

RAIN CLOUDS

Rain that falls
cures and heals
all those who've been broken,
yet never yield.
It purifies the sins of the fallen
and brings light
to those who don't have it.
Seeps into the ground
where it cannot be found.
Deep into the hearth
of our rebirth.
Sings songs that calm
the soul into peacefulness.
Makes it whole
with no other goal.
Take the rain
and enjoy it while it lasts,
for it brings with it our renewal.
Yet, when it drops its final tear,
so die our cheers.

Elvira S. Castillo
12th Grade
La Joya High School
Sullivan City, TX

MOON

My moon's salty tears
Push and pull her tides on Earth
She hides her beautiful craters
From our eyes
In embarrassment

Her heavenly glow,
Acting as a muse for millennia,
She labels as "boring" and "trivial"
While pointing to her rival

Her enemy, the spherical, fiery
Manifestation of humanity's burning passion
The overbearing, scalding heat he exudes
Tortures our skin, melting our brains

Yet, she envies his power
The Sun, the deity
Revered by humanity, as well,
For his never-ending source of life
Aware even she
Would be meaningless without him

But my love has never owned a mirror
Her perfection manifests with every
Graceful twirl on her axis
Blind to the virtue of simplicity
Ignorant of the pain
Of the murderous intent of his passion

For I know
My burnt heart is nowhere safer

Than her protective embrace

**Ananda Nandigam
12th Grade
Science Academy of South Texas
San Juan, TX**

LIGHT

Looking up and seeing darkness
It's spreading until I can't see
And it's heading towards me
I have to run until I'm free

The tunnel is closing
Growing smaller and smaller
Not wanting to let me out
I keep wanting to shout
I'm alone and you can't hear a sound
That means I can't be found
I have to let myself out
And I'll have to do it somehow

I run 'til my legs hurt
Until I hear something and I'm alert
But it's just the thoughts in my head
Asking *why can't I just be dead*

Then I see it, the light
Maybe it's fire or sunshine
Whatever it may be
I have to go to it before the darkness finds me

My eyes focused on one thing
The light that is going to set me free
I have to find it before it's too late
I can't make that same mistake

There it is, I found it
It's waiting for me
I can't wait to see what's out there
I hope there isn't any loneliness or despair

I close my eyes and wait
I feel something in me, I'm awake
All I see are the bright lights
And no more dark nights
The light leads me to freedom
And I can't thank it enough
For it has helped me in more ways than one
I feel amazing, like I can do anything
And I owe it to the light, for my life now means something

Eyden Gonzalez
8TH Grade
Sharyland North High School
Mission, TX

LA LLAMA

Cuando veo hacia afuera al sol, la luna y las estrellas
me pregunto cuánto vale el afán de esta vida
si hay miles de personas y sólo soy una más

¿Cuánto vale lo que haga?
¿Cuánto vale el estrés y la preocupación
si dejo a un lado todo lo más importante?

La vida es una rutina
de la que ya cansada estoy.
Viene la noche y luego la mañana
y hay que hacer lo mismo todos los días
lo mismo

La llama que antes pensaba que estaba dentro de mí
se apaga lentamente.
Y sólo queda el humo de la esperanza
que antes tuve
de la ilusión por un nuevo amanecer.

El mundo que antes miraba lleno de luz y de sueños
ahora sólo es
descolorido.
Y todo pierde sentido
y me desvanezco entre la persona que soy
y la persona que quiero ser.

Me siento impotente
dentro de mí hay un anhelo
que arde por poder alcanzarte
por llegar a ti
porque mi vida signifique algo
por saber a dónde voy

y qué será de mí.

Tengo la necesidad de renacer
de ser alguien nueva
de encontrarme a mí misma.
Que prenda la luz dentro de mí
como una estrella en la noche oscura
y alumbre a todo mi alrededor
y llene mi ser, mi alma
mi vida
con colores nuevos
con esperanzas nuevas
con sueños nuevos.
Y entonces podré recuperar la ilusión
y la llama volverá a arder.

Cesia Hernández
10th Grade
La Joya Early College High School
Peñitas, TX

POST-BREAKUP

Pardon, I pray I won't annoy –
but I am not a toy.

I forgive you
despite no breakthrough
as to why you find me funny –
my eyes are no longer sunny.
I feel so sad, perhaps even mad,
when I think of how I care for thou.

When I think
of laughs and winks,
I implore no more contorts.

For you have this power, a powerful power –
great, doubtful and dower!

For with you, I can shine and I can wine,
both of which I don't do fine.

But that's alright, I'll stay and fight!
Perhaps I can win thee over
once again.

All to know her
and her shine within.

Samuel David Alonso Jr.
10th Grade
San Benito High School
San Benito, TX

LA FLOR

Hasta la flor más marchita renace
sin importar lo deprimida y caída que se ve, resurgirá.
Las nubes pueden cubrir los rayos del sol
pero nunca serán tantas para cubrir un rayo de esperanza.
Podrán traer oscuridad donde hace falta la luz del sol
pero también traen esa agua que necesitas para crecer.
La tormenta puede parecer que durará mucho tiempo…
"KRAKA-BUUUM" se escuchan los truenos.
El viento puede moverte de un lado hacia el otro
llegando hasta el punto de pensar que tu tallo no podrá soportar y quebrará
pero después de la tormenta se despeja todo trayendo ese rayito que necesitabas
y justo igual que las flores renacerás.

Luis Enrique Garza
10th Grade
La Joya Early College High School
Peñitas, TX

UNA VEZ MAS

Me encontraste cuando ni yo misma pude.
En medio de la tormenta,
ahí estabas cuidando mi ser.
Pero de tierra estaba cubierta por completa
mis ojos ciegos quedaron y llenos de maldad.

Y aun así decidiste amarme como nunca.
Hice todo para comprobar que no soy Digna,
Llore con mis pulmones de fuera, llena de dolor.
Oh, pero tu misericordia me alcanzo
del exterior hasta lo interior.

Fuertemente estiraste tus brazos hacia mi
tristemente como el agua entre mis manos
una vez más lo hice.
Una vez más comprobé que no merezco nada.
Con dolor, una vez más te falle
y me equivoque en hacerlo.

Te rechace sin pensar y como una inútil me tropecé.
Claro, como siempre, lastimándote y desviándome en mi propio camino.
cuando pensé que podía terminar esta carrera,
no pude más y me dejé llevar.
Pero me amaste tanto que aun tu misericordia me alcanzo.

Sofia Elizondo
12th Grade
La Joya Early College High School
Palmview, TX

ONCE AGAIN

You found me when even I couldn't.
In the middle of my storm,
there you were taking care of my soul.
I was completely covered in dust,
my blind eyes filled with wicked ideas.

And yet, you loved me like never before.
I did everything to prove I am not worthy.
I cried my lungs out, full of pain.
Oh, how your mercy reached
from my exterior to my interior.

You stretched your strong arms out to me.
Sadly, like water running between my hands,
I did it once again.
With pain, I failed you
and messed up by doing so.

I rejected you without thinking and tripped.
Always hurting you and going my own way.
Just when I thought I'd finish the race,
I couldn't continue.
But your love and mercy reached out to me again.

Sofia Elizondo
12th Grade
La Joya Early College High School
Palmview, TX

S.O.S

9-1-1
No one's answering
I think I am done
I began suffering

Can't see anything
No one even caring
Gone in a ding
Without any repairing

Feeling everything numb
Something is happening
They are calling my mum
And now, everything is darkening

Seeing the light
Then got woken up
I won the fight
And I know I have been taken care of

Lizbeth Leal
11th Grade
La Joya Early College High School

FELIZ

Cortadas aún más profundas, una tras otra.
Me dijiste "Sé feliz, Quizás no vuelva".
Lo intenté, de verdad lo intenté.
Pero cuando lo descubriste
me dijiste "Esa no es la salida."

Siempre pensé cómo lo haces,
ser feliz, es difícil.
Lo descubrí; fingir todo.
Tóxico fue todo lo de alrededor.
Ahora miento sobre mi felicidad.

Un día más, un día más sin dejar de llorar...
Un día más, una marca más...
Un día más, más noches sin dormir.
Ahora no quiero dormir
por miedo de no despertar,
por miedo de no ver tus ojos un día más

Un día más, un comienzo nuevo,
un nuevo ver, ya no es igual.
El llanto de todos los días ahora es una risa,
una risa como el cantar de un pájaro.
El brillar como el resplandor del sol,
tus ojos como ese resplandor,
un resplandor que te hace tener paz.

Ahora río sin parar,
ahora tengo un nuevo comienzo.
Ahora sueño,
sueño nuevos pensamientos.
Ahora soy feliz sin batallar,
Ahora no hay otra salida más que la felicidad.

Nunca más escondida en la tristeza,
una tristeza que acaba,
pero una felicidad que te da un nuevo vivir.

Saraí López
10th Grade
La Joya Early College High School
Peñitas, TX

TEMPTING FIRE

Hot! BLAZING! Scorching hot! Keeping my hand in the fire. It is a choice, not a necessity. I chose to irrationally make a decision that could alter my life for better or worse. My skin starts to bubble. I keep my hand in, then choose to stick in the other. Why? Because I am not thinking. I do without thinking. My skin begins to melt. I continue, even though it hurts, making me scream and cry. I refuse to listen. I refuse to follow instructions, so the product explodes on my face. I am stubborn, so I get angry because I know the fire blazing inside me is greater than the fire that destroys my body on the outside. Covering my eyes, thinking the pain will stop, but surprised it doesn't. At this point, I am so ruined, so hurt, I know I can't turn back now. I'm so destroyed, and in pieces, and on the ground. Down to the bone. I decide there's no use. So I become furious and force myself, with the very little strength I have left, to jump into the fire. I choose to. My decision. We make our own choices knowing there will be consequences. So don't be like me, and stay away from the tempting fire.

Juliana Perez
11th Grade
Rio Grande High School
Rio Grande, TX

II. Flight

"Life is not measured by the number of breaths we take, but by the moments that take our breath away."
-Maya Angelou

THE WEIGHT

Wandering the woods can be a pleasure,
with no end to be measured.
Down she goes the winding trail.
No destination in mind,
just wants to leave the past behind.

She hears the cries of the wind calling her name,
but decides to make her own way.
Down she goes the winding trail.
The difficult path she has taken
is not to be mistaken.

She carries the weight of those she has touched,
for they have given her quite some trouble.
She must now make up for it on the double.
Down she goes the winding trail.
The problems have been fixed,
yet she tires of this game.
Mountains weigh her down,
while her companions are light as a feather.
They don't notice her struggle.
She is bound to collapse,
one way or another.

As her destination is set
and her resolve is finally steeled,
she knows what must be done.
Here comes the end of her winding trail.
Now she smiles,
for the gods have spoken.
The weight thrusted upon her
has now been taken.

She broke the chains that dragged her down.

Her wings have spread and are taking flight.
No one can hold her down tonight.

**Elvira S. Castillo
12th Grade
La Joya High School
Sullivan City, TX**

SAME OLD LIES

Same old stories, same old lies
None of it is worth it,
who will be next to die?
Whom can I trust
when everyone hides behind a disguise?
Every corner I turn is full of deceit
If I believe it, there lies my demise
There's nowhere to run
There's nowhere to hide
I'm just done

Same old stories, same old lies
None of its worth it,
might as well die.
No one is loyal,
whom can we trust?
To most, loyalty seems worthless,
but lies are a must.
God knows what happened to the truth
And we are all at fault
For we all ate part of the forbidden fruit

Same old stories, same old lies
None of it is worth it,
I might as well die.
In this world full of cruelty
I lost the faith of those around me
Darkness and shadows try to engulf me
But I found a way to set my soul free
I found a ray of light
It may be small,
but it gave me the will to fight.
This spark has grown,

and this fire lives inside.

How it came to me is unknown,
but I'm glad it's there.

Same old stories, same old lies
None of it is worth it,
so I learned to fly.

Elvira S. Castillo
12 Grade
La Joya High School
Sullivan City, TX

WINGS

Don't fall from the sky
I don't wanna be afraid
I am going up high
So all that fear will go into a fade

Now it's my time
To be brave
It's not a crime
To misbehave

Cold, Cold, Cold
I can't take it
Can't even soar
But I know I can make it

Aspiration
Is what this brings
And inspiration
For these wings

Lizbeth Leal
11th Grade
La Joya Early College High School

RENACIDA

Hoy siento el poder o el derecho
de actuar,
hablar
o pensar como quiero,
viva, hermosa, sensacional.

Hoy me levanto
como un ave fénix
renacida de las sombras oscuras
bellamente moldeada en
regocijo.

Hoy está aquí, no me aferraré
a el ayer.

Fabiola Chávez
10th Grade
La Joya Early College
La Joya, TX

REBIRTH

Today I feel the power or right
to act
speak
or think as I want -
vivid, beautiful, sensational

Today I'll rise
like a phoenix
reborn from the dark shadows
beautifully pieced into
exhilaration

Today is here, I will not
cling
to yesterday!

Fabiola Chávez
10th Grade
La Joya Early College
La Joya, TX

THE LIAR

Please, I beg of you! Lord, can't you show pity?
Perhaps I've been rude... not witty.
But why must I apologize
when afterwards I'll simply be chastised?
No!
I will not submit to your sickened song.
After all, to lie is to do wrong.
Thus, in a sense, I am far more correct.
So don't you suspect
that I'll be back.

Samuel David Alonso Jr.
10th Grade
San Benito High School
San Benito, TX

BARTEND HER

Margarita yells for me today
like she's lost all her eyesight.
She's sweating in front of me
and wants so desperately
for me to kiss her brow.
I want her to leave, but
I'm the one who invited her over,
and she's only been here a short while.
It would be rude of me
to call the stranger who
hitchhiked over here to me.
"We can't see each other anymore."
I imagine myself saying those words,
like I'm on a roller coaster ride -
and saying them would stop me
from rolling over the peak of the hill.
But part of me wants to whisper it
on the last second,
and purposefully roll over and ride.
Enjoying everything for a mere second,
then throwing up.
First my food.
Then my memories.
Then my guts.
She's sitting in front of me, still.
My Margarita on the rocks,
patiently waiting for a move,
a kiss, a sip...
My co-workers gaze and ask me if I am all right.
I cannot hear them anymore.
I make out with Margarita
kike she's the last thing I'll ever touch before I die.
She was.

After she left
through the back door
of my mouth,
I kept inviting her back.
And each time.
it was almost as if
her makeup looked better -
earrings dangled nicer,
umbrella glowing brighter
under the black lights.
I looked at her
like she was the last thing I'd look at
before I died.
She was.
I did.

Krista A. Olivarez
12th Grade
Veterans Memorial High School
Mission, TX

THE CLOUD

Sheer heartbreak, my world ripped in two halves
The utmost betrayal of the beholder of my heart
Trickles of blood spilled from my chest
Tears of pain flowed from my burning eyes
The sinking feeling of a weight
shoved down my throat
Chained my thoughts to the depth of my self-hatred

Sometimes I could look up
And see a cloud
A beautiful, white cloud
Floating with no purpose, no direction
But heavenly to my hurting eyes

Always changing, always morphing
From a summer's day to a raging thunderstorm
It is there

Floating

No knowledge of the trembling figure 6 feet below it

That night, the fires of my heart were burning me alive
As I panted out of exhaustion and frustration
As I sobbed, the red droplets filled my hands
Then I felt a raindrop splatter on the back of my neck

And another

And another

I slowly looked up as the green fires waned
The rain washed away the bruises and cuts of my heart

The cooling relief was almost too much to bear
I yelled my thanks and words of appreciation at the cloud
But it was too far away to hear

Ananda Nandigam
12th Grade
Science Academy of South Texas
San Juan, TX

PHOENIX

Beautiful and stunning wings
Bright red and orange feathers
But, it wasn't always this way
It grows into it on a very special day

A small baby phoenix is out in the world
But, they call it ugly and disgusting
One person decides to take care of it
Helping it grow bit by bit

Day after day, the little bird never grew
No matter what they did
The little bird just stared back
As if it was in a flashback

'Til one day, it exploded to show its bright colors
Shots of red, orange, and yellow
Moving every which way
Just like fireworks on New Year's Day

The caretaker was blown away
Thinking and thinking about what to do or say
They kept thinking they were crazy, seeing things
So they killed the poor little bird, pulling apart the wings

But, the bird didn't disappear
It was once again just a little bird
Looking at the caretaker, again and again
While they were looking at the bloodstain

Crazy and crazy thoughts went through their head
Thinking about how the bird was just dead
But no explanation

They thought it was just a hallucination

One day, the bird did it again
Except this time, it flew away
Flying to its next destination
Where it will be reborn as just another hallucination

Eyden Gonzalez
8th Grade
Sharyland North
Mission, TX

BLOOM

When she flutters her eyelids, you could almost swear
You hear the heartbeat of a butterfly's wings
Or see her shy violet lashes
Bloom

Krista A. Olivarez
12th Grade
Veterans Memorial High School
Mission, TX

RENACIMIENTO

Renacimiento: recuperar o renovar la fuerza, la energía o el
cansancio significa cuando una persona nace de nuevo
o se siente como una nueva persona.

Yo me siento libre y con libertad,
como una nueva persona,
hoy me siento que puedo ser todo porque soy nacida de
nuevo.

Hoy no debe darse por sentado.
Hoy no es prometido ni dado,
por esa razón yo me levanto con gracia,
como una marmota despertando de la hibernación.

Hoy me levanto con entusiasmo
como un gallo en la mañana,
o como cuando el día sigue floreciendo bendiciones.

Hoy está aquí, no dependeré de ayer,
soy una nueva persona.
Y no miraré hacia atrás.

Grecia A. Elizondo
10th grade
La Joya Early College High School
Peñitas, TX

III. Growth

*"Let us gather in a flourishing way
with sunluz grains abriendo los cantos
que cargamos cada día — "*
-Juan Felipe Herrera

TEEN MIND

Not understanding
Not getting it
Not surprising
Not gonna sweat it

Very Tired
Just wanna rest
I'll end up getting fired
This is not even the best

The real world
Has its times
The minute you turn
You see the lights & fights

The strongest minds
Have the deepest stories
We don't understand what's going on
It can be depressing or a glory

Lizbeth Leal
11th Grade
La Joya Early College High School

RENACIMIENTO

Algo hermoso que nace dentro nuestro corazón,
una flor floreciendo por primera vez dentro el alma
donde el mundo convierte la muerte en vida.
Recuperación de la fuerza encuentra lo mejor.
Llama de amor viva que tiernamente hiere a mi alma
en el más profundo centro
donde se encuentran errores y decepciones
que ahora sólo son recuerdos.
Zarcillos de tristeza que llegan más profundo.
En ese lugar al lado de mi alma que ha muerto
donde grito silenciosamente sin aliento.
Tímidamente mirando hacia fuera
para un día ver el sol otra vez.
Y lo único que queda son las cicatrices de batalla.

Isaura Castillo
11th Grade
La Joya Early College High School
La Joya, TX

MODERNIZACIÓN

Modernización puede ocurrir en una cultura
con las tradiciones o con las ideas,
hay tantas cosas que en este día han cambiado
como las leyes, tecnología y más.
Con las cosas buenas vienen las malas
como la renovación de armas y la forma de lucha
en comparación con antes
cuando usaban arcos y flechas y de eso fue mosquete
todo con la idea de matar más eficientemente.
Pero lo bueno con todo esto es la tecnología que puede
salvar vidas y también hay nuevos entendimientos del
mundo.
Y con cada día que pasa hay nuevas cosas
que quieren ser encontradas y personas que quieren
encontrarlas.

Ángel Guerra
10th Grade
La Joya Early College High School
Peñitas, TX

RENOVACIÓN

Quisiera ser una mejor persona,
los de me rodean no son buenas personas,
quizás eso es el problema,
culpar a los demás no cambiará nada,
pero en verdad quisiera cambiar yo,
no por nadie,
sólo por mí misma,
una persona buena como mi mamá,
tal vez un cambio sería mejor,
mi madre muy buena siempre es con la gente,
mi madre es muy noble con los demás,
cómo quisiera tener su nobleza,
cómo quisiera ser así de buena,
no tengo paciencia para la gente,
no tengo tolerancia para las tonterías de otros,
solamente quiero ser buena persona y sé que se puede,
pero que lo haré no estoy segura...

Karina Montoya
10th Grade
La Joya Early College High School
Peñitas, TX

DIFFICULT RENOVATION

The time has sadly come
to finally renovate my home,
most difficult thing I've ever had to do.

To think about all the memories
that happened here,
makes it more difficult.
The biggest moments...
my first steps
times my family fought
made up
and made stronger bonds
made new friends
had good times
celebrated all of the holidays and birthdays here.

Since I can remember,
this has been the place.
When I think of
all the great things that happened here,
it's like heaven.

And now have to throw it all away,
this couldn't be any harder!

Omar Venegas
10th Grade
La Joya Early College High School
La Joya, TX

RENOVACIÓN DIFÍCIL

El momento ha llegado tristemente,
para finalmente renovar mi casa,
es lo más difícil que he tenido que hacer.
Pensar en todos los recuerdos que transitaron aquí,
lo está haciendo aún más difícil.
Las cosas más grandes pasaron aquí,
mis primeros pasos,
las familias lucharon,
arreglaron sus problemas,
e hicieron lazos más fuertes.
Hice nuevos amigos,
tuve buenos tiempos,
celebramos todas las fiestas y cumpleaños allí,
desde que recuerdo que este ha sido el lugar,
cuando piensas en todas las grandes cosas que sucedieron
allí,
es como el cielo
y ahora hay que tirarlo todo.
¡Esto no podría ser más difícil!

Omar Venegas
10th Grade
La Joya Early College High School
La Joya, TX

THINKING LIKE FLOWERS

I try to think less
The less I think the less I stress
I try to avoid my state of mind
I'm so afraid of myself, I tend to hide
from the person holding the evil eye
It is blind, but you can see it
Jealousy maybe?
I'm not sure, but I sense it
I see it in your face when you're behind
The more I see, the more it is lined
But why?
Hate will never win
For you will never defeat me
Of all the things I might be,
I'm nothing compared to you.
You're a part of me
and still far from me
Yes, I am you
and yes, you are me
We are not the same, can't you see?
You're the part of me I don't like to show
Yet you take advantage of me at night when I'm alone
You're the part of me
thinking everyone's looking at you
And you're the part of me believing
everything people say about you is true
You convince yourself you are not worth it
You feel like you are in a dead end, you feel deserted
That's where I take over
I take control and make sure I'm sober
I've fought this side of me and now it's gone
It's away
I'm just glad to say I'm okay

I'm like roses with thorns
I've blossomed into something new, I've been reborn

Kayla De León
10th Grade
La Joya Early College High School
La Joya, TX

PENSANDO COMO LAS FLORES

Trato de pensar menos,
cuanto menos pienso, menos estrés siento.
Intento evitar mi estado de ánimo
tengo tanto miedo que tiendo a esconderme
de la persona que sostiene el mal de ojo.
Está ciega, pero todavía puede verlo.
¿Celos tal vez?
no estoy segura, pero lo siento.
Lo veo en tu cara cuando estás detrás,
cuanto más veo, más se alinea
pero por qué.
El odio nunca ganará
porque nunca me vencerás
y después de todas las cosas podría ser yo.
pero no soy nada comparada contigo.
Eres parte de mí
pero aún estás lejos de mí
si yo soy tu
y si tú eres yo
pero no somos la misma, ¿no ves?
eres la parte de mí que no me gusta mostrar.
Sin embargo, te aprovechas de mí por la noche cuando estoy sola.
Eres la parte de mí que piensa que todos te miran.
Y tú eres la parte de mí que piensa que todo lo que la gente dice sobre ti es verdad.
Te convences de que no vales la pena.
Te sientes como si estuvieras en un callejón sin salida, te sientes desierto
y ahí es donde me hago cargo.
Tomo el control y me aseguro de estar sobria.
He luchado contra este lado de mí y ahora se ha ido.
Está lejos.
Me alegra decir que estoy bien,

soy como las rosas con espinas.
Me he convertido en algo nuevo, he renacido.

**Kayla De León
10th Grade
La Joya Early College High School
La Joya, TX**

FORBIDDEN FRUIT

I loved a woman with the passion
of a burning fire in the rain.
She had a name and mind I can't remember,
and came with the figure of an hourglass
that had sand already running out.

He then asked me "*How could you love her?*"
as he stared at me like a
father stares at his lying child.
"*If the only time you spent,*" he continued,
"*you were naked, and thereafter ashamed?*"

He left me to think
- alone -
"I didn't know," I reasoned with myself.
"How could I?"
He angrily flew down and exclaimed
"*You did know, for I told you!
YOU ate the fruit of the flesh
for the flavor, and not the wisdom*"

"I did love her," I lied to his face.
"I was naked, was I not?" The sin peeled off my mouth.
"*You were naked, yet clothed.*"
He lifted his hand to say
"*May sin and flesh be your father now.*"

**Samuel David Alonso Jr.
10th Grade
San Benito High School
San Benito, TX**

VAMPIRE TEETH

Have you seen his grin...
how it's crooked and vile?
To think of all his sin
kept within a smile!

Oh, how he prays,
and forces his gaze...
like a maze, his daze delays
- and stays.

He dresses stupid
and his actions are odd.
With a mind always lucid,
some say he's a fraud.

I've never seen him cry!
That I find odd,
to say the least.
Yes, he must be a beast!

As well, he talks too much.
He cares and such.
Oh, sir vampire,
with your ruined teeth.

It is sad,
how your smile scares
- at times, ensnares.

It captivates,
but you do not.
You exacerbate and differentiate
with a skull that burns red hot.

I am the vampire.
My esteem grows no higher.
But I pray so that one day you'll see
a deeper part of me.

Samuel David Alonso Jr.
10th Grade
San Benito High School
San Benito, TX

MOTHER AND MAN

Trees flow wistfully
under the cover of a blackened sky.
Reaching for what cannot be grasped,
with branches masquerading
as macabre hands.
Leaves fly restlessly across every other sad burst of breeze
Searching for a place to land
Where the grass shows the little life they now have.
Amongst the quiet war of greenery and wind,
a man reminisces upon an open field.
He recalls the wisdom he once upheld
but like the color of summer trees,
his leaves were caught on a wayward gust
of anxious Autumn changes that force all to fall.
The once proud man finds himself pinned
on starving, chiding blades of grass that could not yield,

for they've tasted leaves on withered skin.
His hollowed bones give way to dust
after the youth he still held escaped his husk.
Standing tall in front of the wicked greenery,
the boy enforced his new mark of majesty.

Eras pass and much is gone,
the boy's reign continued.
Grass no longer belittled the old leaves -
for nature had long since taken her leave.
Green was traded for black animosity,
blue rage, and grey indifference
by the boy and his people
who scoffed at the old world's primitiveness.
Never would the old wise man return

from the deepest reaches of the Earth
to show the boy love and compassion -
what he has not received since rebirth.

Andrew Van Wagoner
12th Grade
Pioneer High School
Palmhurst, TX

ONE MORE DAY

Brisk fresh night
Sirens echoed through the street
For somehow, they thought he was okay
Little did they know they were so wrong
Victim of rape at only ten
"Murder. Rape. It's just a shot away," he thought
The voices
The oh-so tantalizing voices
Multiple antidepressants
Lexapro
Xanax
Abilify
Zoloft
Nothing ever seemed to work
Staring at the blank, white wall in utter despair
He heard his mother talking to him
but couldn't hear anything except the voices

Writing his goodbye letter
He thanked his mom for giving birth to him though he was
ungrateful for his life
I'm writing this letter to say goodbye
Please don't miss me
Please don't cry
As he grabbed the bottle of prescription pills marked
XANAX
He opens the bottle
he runs his fingers along the ridged edges of the bottle
He set the letter on the medicine cabinet
He swallows as much as he can in a handful
Hands cold
Dizzy
Slow breaths
Blackness

Wakes up in a hospital bed
Regretting he wanted to be dead
Tubes in his throat and tears in his eyes
Happy to have not met his demise
Today he is happy to be whom he is
Reborn and happy to this day
This is the only thing he had to say
Do not think about the past
Think about the stuff that lasts
Get through it day by day
Because nothing is more important
than what you have to say

Joel A. Sanchez
9th Grade
Sharyland Pioneer High School
Mission, TX

PUZZLE

She has fought wars in her head
Battles in her heart
Scars on her hands
And blood on her arms

Smiles are brave
Tears are strong
She has fought back
But hasn't won

She wants real smiles
She wants love
Not from her head
But from her heart

She is glass, shattered
A million pieces
Slowly being repaired
To form one piece that fits together

**Eyden Gonzalez
8th Grade
Sharyland North High School
Mission, TX**

MARY

Mary is a girl with big dreams
And so much hope hidden within her
She makes peace with all of her sorrow
And she has the will to live 'til tomorrow

May was always next to Mary
Telling her things she should believe
Whispers and whispers from behind
But, it just wasn't the right kind

Mary tried not to listen to May
But May's offers were too good to be true
She had to know if she should
But she didn't know if she even could

May never left Mary
Never left her thoughts
Never left her heart
All of which are Mary's most important parts

Mary always hid behind her bright smile
But, it was getting harder to do
May told her she wasn't good enough
But Mary knew she was tough

Mary was told she wasn't beautiful
May said no one loves her
No one would ever treat her like a human
Because she was just a piece of nothing

Mary grew sad and started to cry
But, May still never left her side
Only to say Mary looked ugly when she cried
And that people don't like that, especially guys

Mary started to believe May, she felt she was right
She soon started to feel numb
May's comments were just a part of her life
The one she left behind

Mary decided one day she needed to feel
So she hurt herself, May saying that was best
On and on she did, until emotion was what she expressed
But it was just pain
She felt, again and again

Soon, she was covered in scars she named feelings
Tons and tons of feelings
May kept encouraging it
Saying she couldn't live without it

One night, Mary read a love letter from someone she loved, she truly did
May said it was just a joke and fake
And to not choose them because it was a mistake

Mary really liked this person, she loved them, it was real true love
Mary, for once, was really sad
So she got mad, and argued with May
All night and all day

Mary was sick and finally decided
She was done with May
So May went back into her head
For that's where she should have always been

Eyden Gonzalez
8th Grade
Sharyland North High School
Mission, TX

BETWEEN THE LINES

There you were, across the table
Across the classroom where I'd find
Myself not present between the lines of your mind
In contrast, me having you in my head
Every day, the picture of you instead
Of something else productive
You, sitting there, conductive of my sight
Every day I'd try to fight
Myself, and my mind, with you between lines in my mind
Your own presence
Has taken me away from the present
Looking for a present
Of your presence right next to me in the present
But that rollercoaster ride is long gone
Me trying to make sense
Trying to keep holding on since
And in my defense
You're between the lines between my mind
To which you will find
A battlefield filled with miles of mines
Mines in the lines between my mind
To which I will find
When you're here all along
I try to rush towards a song or any sound
To have my thoughts and your voice drown out
To ponder my life choices and regrets
While keeping me distracted from them
So yes, oh yes, you may sit there across the table
Across the classroom
With your very own room and space
As I look at your face
I am reminded of our inevitable fate
Which has been ended
And I have defended

The thoughts and actions of my life
While you sit there between the lines of my mind
It may seem fine
All that weight after our fate
But it's having me wait
For a specific date
For a time where a meaningful word
One that won't go unheard
One that won't lead to a third try
You left all your chances on the floor
Didn't even bother picking up three or four
Therefore leaving us to our fate
That has got me thinking about it to this day
If something else happened
If it would have had a different end
But either way, I'd STILL depend on you
I'm biding, yes, biding my time
For the time you slip from between the lines
Out of my mind
And find my backbone growing
Showing that my mind is fine
But until that time
You're still here in my mind
Racing between the lines
While I'm biding my time
Even so
All I can do is cope
And hope one day
I'll grow a spine and fly away
From my mind, into my happy place
Forever gone without a trace
Of you or any other thing
That tries to mess with me
And bring me down from my destiny
Ergo
I know that if I undergo my recovery

Into my growing spine that's growing high
That's showing the disappearance of the bold and dark lines
in my mind
You'll be gone
And without a trace
My present is your absence
Of your presence
In between the lines that lay comfortably
In the skyscraper that is my mind
And it's not moving anytime soon

Joram Cuanang
10th Grade
Sharyland Advanced Academic Academy
Mission, TX

VISION

Vision,
my vision of you lets me know you're respectful,
it reveals you're unique.

Vision,
my vision of you lets all know you're irrational,
it reveals you're distinctive.

Vision,
the vision that says I'm perfect,
the one that shows I am too good to be true.

Vision,
the vision that says that I need help,
I'm imperfect,
I'm surreal.

WE all have a vision,
we all have a weakness,
but we all are the same.

Vision,
the real empathy we feel,
the one that says we're poor,
unsatisfied.

We may commit mistakes,
but we all walk that pathway,
we try to be perfect,
but we all fall and find ourselves to make.

We are not perfect,
we just began our ride,

we just began our...
Vision.

Vanessa Vega
12th Grade
Sharyland High School

IV. Glimpses

"There is no time limit on pain and no expiration date on love."
-Daniel García Ordaz

NOT MY DREAM

I had a dream.

It had love, marriage, kids,
an altogether good life.
But I did not lead the dream,
nor did I appear in it.

Yes, it is true!
I felt another man's strife!
It all seemed like his fear.

That angrily brings me a tear!
Gingerly, I beg to be near
that love, that sorrow, and strife.
Maybe have
a house, son, and wife.

Yet, this man is afraid
of a debt that's unpaid.
And here I remain,
alone and not swayed.

Maybe I can find this man,
try and take his life!
And if I really can?
I'll stay and help his wife.

Have a friend.
Not be alone.
How could it end?
I'll find my own.

I found him...

He's happy, with children running free.
Children who know nothing of me.

And yes, it is true.

I had a dream not new.
Sadly, it seems.
That was not my dream.

Samuel David Alonso Jr.
10th Grade
San Benito High School
San Benito, TX

HANGING OUT ON THE THRESHOLD

I'm trying to figure out
Who the other person
Behind the mirror is.

She won't let me in
Copies me to tease me
All the time
Like she wants to be me
And not herself.

We look alike
Twins
Though we are abundant in difference.

Since I can't figure out
Who she is
And she'd rather be me,
I look at the mirror more often
So we can be the same.

Never having to wonder
Who it is that we are.

Krista A. Olivarez
12th Grade
Veterans Memorial High School
Mission, TX

THE ATTIC

Every picture of *you*
Collects dust
In my head
Until I get to visit
Again at night
And clean them up

Krista A. Olivarez
12th Grade
Veterans Memorial High School
Mission, TX

THE EARLY WORM

The worm locked eyes with the early bird and saw nothing but emptiness.
The worm could not help but wonder whether a good night's rest was worth hunger's sedation.
But then again, he was awake in the early hours of dawn just to see the foolish fowl before him.
The bird had left its nest at five o'clock sharp to fill his stomach's void.
The brave worm that stared at it removed all its feelings of predation,
and instead instilled a curiosity for how such a failure for a serpent could make it feel so dim.

The worm burrowed into the bird's heart and found a soft spot to lie in,
giving it a new aspect of care and compassion for the world it soared above
and allowed it to sleep for well past twelve.
They, together, were early no longer -
for time was something abstract to a worm and his bird.
Time was meaningless and nonexistent.
Time could not loosen the ties of ultimate coexistence.

Andrew Van Wagoner
12th Grade
Pioneer High School
Palmhurst, TX

LOVE

Love is a dream
that can throw you down
or pick you up from the ground
you once were on,
but it can also destroy.
Imagine being a piece of glass
that could be shattered
by a hammer in someone else's hand.
It begins like a love song
that can then be torn into pieces.
Love is like a loyal dog that will stay by your side
or run out and leave you torn.
It causes you to go from a shining star
to a burnt-out flame in the sky.
It feels like summer fun,
'til it's all gone.
Ending up broken hearted or full of joy
is the truth of the love toy.

Yadira Rocha
7th Grade
Grulla Middle School RGCCISD
Grulla, TX

MY GUY

I love a guy
With the biggest smile
I love a guy
With the prettiest eyes
I love a guy
Whose voice can break and make me
I love a guy
Who's here for me
I love a guy
Who will help me stop cutting
I love a guy
Who will never be mine
I love a guy
Who belongs to her
So I loved a guy
Who never loved me

Kendra Cornjeo
8th Grade
Grulla Middle School RGCCISD
Grulla, TX

IT'S NOT

It's not that I cry every night
It's not that I have death in my life
It's not that I'm too suicidal
It's that I'm empty
I'm alone
I don't feel
I'm just a shell of who I used to be
I'm used to all of these feelings
I'm used to being left, pushed aside
I'm used to being hurt
Cheated
Lied to
I'm used to it all
And I'm sick of it all

Kendra Cornjeo
8th Grade
Grulla Middle School RGCCISD
Grulla, TX

PEOPLE

People point out every mistake I make and am
I find myself doing it also
I spend hours pointing things out that are wrong with me
But can't spend five minutes looking at the good
That's what people do
Little do they know they count the stars they lost to the moon

Kendra Cornjeo
7th Grade
Grulla Middle School RGCCISD
Grulla, TX

WHY?

Why?
Why is it I get jealous?
Why is it I can't see you with her?
That I don't want you with other girls?
Why am I so scared you like them?
Why am I so scared you want them?
Why am I so scared of losing you?
I'm so scared of losing you, but you're not mine.
Why are you not scared of losing me?
When I'm so scared of loving you, but you don't love me.
So say sorry to your girl cause now I know how she felt when you first met me.
But I guess it was a routine you do.
You go around making a girl feel loved,
just to turn around and find a new one.

Kendra Cornjeo
8th Grade
Grulla Middle School RGCCISD
Grulla, TX

PROBLEMS

I could drink away my problems
Smoke away the pain
Cut away the cravings
But what would I gain?
After I'm done drinking
Done with the high
Cravings all gone
What was the prize?
I still feel hurt
I still feel pain
After all that
What did I gain?
It didn't do much
Won't do more
It gave me a reason
Now I'm on the floor
I need someone now
Someone who'll stay
Love me for who I am
Not change me in any way
I wish it would end
I wish it were gone
All these emotions
I wish it were done
I wake up every morning
Look in the mirror
Hate what I saw
And wish I would disappear
People see my smile
But my world is upside down
They see what they want
But I see a frown
I try to be hopeful
Try to stay strong
But with the life I have
I turn out to be wrong
I have Big Dreams
Bigger than I could ever see

But people knock me down
Simply because they disagree
Most think I am typical
Think I'm okay
But I am different; unique
In each and every way
I can drink away my problems
I can smoke away the pain
I can cut away the cravings
But I would go insane

Juliana Perez
11th Grade
Rio Grande High School
Rio Grande City, TX

THE STRAY

A stray dog in comparison to me.
It craves food as I crave attention, affection, love.
Began to stare and with innocent, hopeless eyes,
it stares back wanting food from me because I'm all it's
got. The little hope it bares to contain. In relief,
I feel pity and the stray dog knows I do. It is unsure if it
should walk towards a stranger, so it sits and
watches me as I slowly emerge my hand
from my backpack to get a large bottle of milk and bread.
As it continuously stares hesitantly, it fights its legs and
stomach. It keenly steps towards the bread I hold it out in
pity. Once the dog has arrived to my destination,
it nibbles the bread a bit to let me know it has gone
through enough abuse and is scared. As I notice this, I
begin to realize I'm staring at a mirror image. I have
gained enough of its trust that it let me stroke the top of its
head, all the way down to the crippled bones referred to as
a tail. Examining this dog, I see it has cuts along its legs as
I do on my own legs and arms. I see how badly beaten this
stray is, as my own heart has been. Giving it milk, it drinks
in thirst. Eats in hunger. Agrees to let me show it affection.
Once it finishes the milk, it knows it is full. Stomach round,
yet bones are noticeable. I stare at this dog wondering
how could it go through the process of eating.
Is it because it's been hungry for so long it consumes as it
has been consumed? I start to realize this dog is as hurt as
me. Felt pain similar to mine. Is starving even though
it is full. I can't bear to see this dog like this. I pity it as
others would pity me if they knew what I've been through.
I know this dog has been strong enough to live
as long as it has. Has dignity because it held its head up
high as it walked towards me. Has pride because
it thanked me enough to lick my fingers,
then moved on to my face. Is numb because when
I felt its wounds it hardly flinched at all.
I close my eyes...

Think...

Breathe...

Then walk away on four legs.

**Juliana Perez
11th Grade
Rio Grande High School
Rio Grande City, TX**

FLASH BACK

The sweetest smell of mountainous perfume
The grass set with early morning dew
A white glance of shiny mystic light
Specs falling to the ground compact tight
Beautiful cycle of nature
Sights of mysterious creatures
Missing those moments of glee
To where I want to run away and flee
Catching glimpse of the frozen bend
As a little one, I was only ten
Having such freedom given to me
The season's greatest spark of energy
I stood there in brisk, cold, descending flakes
No feeling or sound that it makes
Peaceful, quiet, clear falling figures
Almost as if taking three dimensional pictures
My favorite season of them all
Guess again, no! It isn't fall
Frozen water, icicles shaped as splinters
Yes, you got it! The season is winter

Juliana Perez
11th Grade
Rio Grande High School
Rio Grande City, TX

PHOENIX

The pungent smell of ash.
Wispy, smoky, with hint of fire brash.
Ash reforms against the norm
But every hint shows its warmth.

Novena ends, a spark is lit,
From the ashes rise
scarlet hues not ready to quit.
Iridescent pinion ready to soar,
Onwards, to the ongoing war.

With azure and rouge
lagging behind them,
Eyes sea-blue twinkling like a reflective gem;
As their flare burns brighter
They go on, no matter the cost, like a fighter.

They settle gently, amaranthine legs gripping
tightly to the balustrade.
They quickly dove to the battle at their fastest rate.
They sharply gripped the air
and flew straight through the warrior haze.
They send out their call in a quick fiery blaze.

Amber wisps could be witnessed
from end to end.
They were sending a message;
they weren't here to fight, but to defend.
Defend them from each other, their hate.
Singing its song, the men's hatred dissipated into
nothingness, making them wonder
how they ended up in this state.

Sweet aromas could be smelled,
easing men into clarity.
The men, eyes widening,
knew they were witnessing a rarity.
Their wings slowed their beats until

they would never again come the same.
Yet, elsewhere, a flame.

Jada T.R. Cantu-Cabrera
9th Grade
Sharyland Pioneer High School
Palmhurst, TX

V.   Rise

"You can never have too much sky."
-**Sandra Cisneros**

RISE

Just like the sun every morning,
like bubbles in your soda,
like a balloon full of helium,

I will rise...

I can't be held down.
Unlike Pinocchio,
*I've got no strings
to hold me down*.

I will rise...

For this is merely a battle
and not a war,
I will be strong.

I will rise...

**Nohelí Alejandra González
10th Grade
La Joya Early College High School
Palmview, TX**

THROUGH THE CONCRETE

Lost and found
Like a plant trying to break
through the concrete its being held back by
Learning to adapt and feeling lost in the process
Am I really making any progress?
Attempting to blossom as nature intended

Don't give up just yet!
What if you are right there?
On the edge of your breakthrough?
It might seem hopeless,
but it's not as hopeless as giving up

To be reborn
one must be temporarily stopped
To forget everything, embracing emptiness
Everything you believed in,
including yourself
In order to get through that concrete
you have to see everything
from an entirely new perspective

Diego Flores
10th Grade
La Joya Early College High School
Mission, TX

A TRAVÉS DEL CONCRETO

Perdido y encontrado de nuevo
como una planta que intenta romper el concreto, está siendo frenada,
aprendiendo a adaptarse, pero sintiéndome perdido en el proceso.
¿Realmente estoy haciendo algún progreso?
Intentar florecer, como pretendía la naturaleza.

¡No te rindas todavía! ¿Qué pasa si estás allí?
¿Al borde de tu avance?
Podría parecer sin esperanza
pero no es tan desesperado como rendirse.

Para renacer, uno debe ser detenido temporalmente,
olvidar todo, tener confianza en
todo en lo que creías
incluyéndote
para poder atravesar ese concreto.

Tienes que ver todo desde una perspectiva totalmente nueva.

Diego Flores
10th Grade
La Joya Early College High School
Mission, TX

THE CALM BEFORE THE STORM

As a new day came about, so did I.
The days turned from ominous clouds to
bright, yellow sunflowers. Colors plastered
around me, which brought unimaginable joy.

A joy I hadn't felt in a while.
A joy that departed years ago and
left the train station long
before I could say goodbye.

Left me stranded with an unspeakable sadness
that caused so much agony.
My life painted with unlikable, ill-lit colors
like ominous clouds on rainy days.

My days turned from a sea of happiness
to a tsunami of sadness. Coming at me
with rapid speed.

As the darkening days have passed,
I have learned to love myself again.
My days no longer seem like a whirlwind of sadness,
but rather a sheet of winding joy.

Miranda Aguayo
10th Grade
La Joya Early College High School
La Joya, TX

LA CALMA ANTES DE LA TORMENTA

Cuando llegó un nuevo día, también lo hice yo.
Los días pasaron de nubes siniestras a
brillantes girasoles amarillos. Colores enlucidos
a mi alrededor, que trajeron alegría inimaginable.

Una alegría que no había sentido en mucho tiempo.
Una alegría que se fue hace años.
Dejó la estación de tren, mucho
antes de que pudiera decir adiós.

Me dejó varada con una tristeza indescriptible.
Eso causó tanta agonía.
Mi vida pintada con colores desagradables, poco iluminados
como nubes siniestras en los días de lluvia.

Mis días pasaron de ser un mar de felicidad
a un tsunami de tristeza. Viniendo a mí
con velocidad rápida.

Como van pasado los días de oscurecimiento,
he aprendido a amarme una vez más.
Mis días ya no parecían un torbellino de tristeza
pero más bien una hoja de alegría sinuosa.

Miranda Aguayo
10th Grade
La Joya Early College High School
La Joya, TX

RENACIMIENTO: EL SONIDO

BOOM! Fuel el sonido,
el sonido de la realidad.
Un sonido que te hace despertar del error,
el error que hemos estado viviendo.

 BOOM! El sonido que se escucha al despertar, un sonido,
que está fuera de lugar.
Luego el sonido después de la tormenta, un silencio total.
Después de llorar, viene la tranquilidad.
Una tranquilidad que te hace pensar,
pensar todo lo que has hecho mal.

A veces ese mal te hace regresar a la realidad,
una realidad que te hace que renazcas.
Renazcas para ser alguien más,
un renacimiento que hace que pienses diferente,
que te hace olvidar todo el mal de tus errores.

Saraí López
10th Grade
La Joya Early College High School
Peñitas, TX

RENACIMIENTO: VOLVER A NACER

Renacimiento significa volver a nacer.
El renacimiento de alguien
es volver a vivir otra vez, pero esta vez haciendo o
creyendo algo nuevo.

Renacimiento es un cambio que ocurre.
Puede ser el renacimiento de una nueva mentalidad
y la oportunidad de aprender nuevas cosas.
El renacimiento puede ser el renacimiento de un nuevo
período.

Hasta puede ser como el renacimiento de una nueva
religión,
puede ser un movimiento cultural.
Puedes pensar de renacimiento como una nueva
oportunidad de hacer las cosas diferentes y dejar el pasado
atrás.
Borrón y cuenta nueva.

Amanda Chapa
11th Grade
La Joya Early College High School
Peñitas, TX

RENACIMIENTO PARA REDENCIÓN

Una nueva vida dada.
Pero no devuelta
porque un viejo hábito nunca se olvida.
Sin embargo, a la persona se le da redención.

Una oportunidad de arreglar errores pasados
o crear nuevos problemas.
La decisión depende de un solo ser.
Pero puede afectar a todo un planeta.

Todo a una persona
para ser gobernada por la codicia
o por la justicia
su acción dirigida por el juicio.
Aunque la mente se nubla con la tentación.

Dada la posibilidad de redimirse.
Pero el pasado todavía puede ser inquietante.
La elección de un humano.
Decidida por su propia voluntad
la persona recibe redención.

Érick Gonzáles
9th Grade
La Joya Early College High School
Peñitas, TX

RENAISSANCE FOR REDEMPTION

A new life given
But not returned
For an old habit never forgotten
Yet the person is given redemption

A chance to fix past mistakes
Or create new problems
The choice is up to a single being
But can affect a whole planet

All is up to one person
To be ruled by greed
Or by justice
Their action led by judgement
Though the mind is clouded with temptation

Given a chance to redeem themselves
The past can still be haunting
The choice of a human
Decided by one's own free will
The person is given redemption

Érick Gonzáles
9th Grade
La Joya Early College High School
Peñitas, TX

ERRONEOUS PERCEPTION

When you look at me
you see dumb,
you see deaf,
and you see crazy.
But I am none of those.
That's just what YOU see.

And while it is true
that I do act and look like all of those things,
those adjectives do not define me.
They only define your erroneous perception of me.

I am creative.
I am curious.
I am inquisitive.
And my mind is never quiet.

I have lots of things going on in my head,
though my blank stare suggests subnormal intellect.

The reality is
I know and use words most people in my grade don't.
I can do math in my head,
and I can learn facts just by listening.

I draw and I listen,
I read and I listen,
I stare at my desk, but I listen.
I examine the things you walk past
without a second thought,
without even a sideways glance.
I notice you snickering at how I act.
How I don't touch the doorknob when I enter the room.
How I have to clean my desk before I sit.

How I share my lunch with the birds
because they don't snicker,
they don't judge.

They just sing their contented songs.

I am not who you think I am
or what you think I'm supposed to be.
I am me.

I can draw my own comic strip.
And erase and redraw,
my brain gushing with ideas of what comes to life on the page.

My eyes see moments
that must be captured
through a camera lens.
Moments that, to you, mean absolutely nothing.
But to me, display the power and beauty of nature.

For you see,
I am not dumb,
I am not stupid,
I am not crazy,
I am simply me.
And in being me,
I apologize for nothing.

Dibany M. Guerra
11th Grade
Sharyland High School
Mission, TX

SCHOOL SNOOZE

I open my eyes in blues
to put that talking clock to snooze.
As though I had to go to school,
my eyes widened to something cool.
The floor was a swamp
with a seven-legged chomp.
I got on its scaly back
and it stopped with a smack.
My house was a JUNGLE!

I saw a tree tower
and a mighty guard waffle with power.
I asked where my school was
as pizzas came out with blue paws,
and we went on a scavenger hunt.

We lost a pizza friend
in a snappy river we befriended.
We swung on gummy vines,
and mine snapped just on time.
I entered a closing portal,
feeling less mortal
as a bulk of pencil came my way.

I snapped each pencil in half
and walked away with a laugh.
A giant butterfly gave me a ride
and dropped me to a clock on its side.
The clock seemed to be a portal
to a world better for mortals.
I walked in, and guess what?!

I saw my school as I sang,

but the dismissal bell rang.

Danaii Elizondo
8th Grade
Grulla Middle School RGCCISD
Grulla, TX

SURVIVAL OF THE FITTEST

Eat, sweat, sore, sleep, repeat. Working out gives me a sense of stability. Pulls me into another dimension. Some people are addicted to drugs, pills, smoking, drinking; however, success is my addiction. Working out is my hobby. School is my job. Family is my life. Jump, squat, push-up, repeat. Sweat dripping fluently down my face... muscles contracting as I push my weight against gravity. Glug, glug, glug ... water running down my esophagus and into my stomach. I'm ready for another set. My muscles are sore with pain... legs shaking with strength. Heart pounding from pumping my blood faster than a cheetah running to kill its prey. I don't give up because I'm not finished. I push myself, I drag myself, and I crawl if I have to get to the finish line. I am my own motivation. I did it. All me. I got myself to the finish line to start a beginning. I jumped with very little strength hoping I would land straight. I sprinted hoping I wouldn't run out of breath. I walked with bruises and wounds. I crawled with broken bones. I kept my head held high knowing everyone around me was *booing* from a distance. You tell me when I die, did I get to the finish line? Did I make it? Was I strong enough? You could only tell me so much, but at the end of the day, I decide to finish or not. Quit or not. I say if I'm finished or not because I myself have gotten this far, so don't tell me I can't. Don't tell me not to. I make my choice. I went through the process of sacrifice. I went through the process of doubt just for people to tell me I can't when I've been pushing myself through my obstacles, one by one. Costing me everything I have given to reach my goals. To do what it has to get to that red ribbon at the end of that circular shaped road because, believe it or not, life is not a straight line. I will strive to accomplish what I believe in because I can. Anything is possible. Those people who are waiting for someone to give them everything. To serve them their career. To make everything easy. What they don't know is life begins when you think you are halfway through. Life is a series of obstacles. Ones you fail at, ones you succeed at, but you are the one to decide to finish or not.

Juliana Perez
11th Grade
Rio Grande High School
Rio Grande City, TX

HEALING

Even after all you have done
Even after all that pain
All those never-ending battles
I'm still living, prospering
Just like the sky after rain

The worst has passed
All that lost hope
Is now brewing and growing
Like a flower in the spring, blooming

All the white nights slowly turning dark
'Til none of the light was left
Is now as bright as the sun
It's all said and done
Warm and loving, no more wanting to run

Most don't find peace
But that wasn't the thing for me
It was very difficult, that is true
That part is lost, but not gone
Because even if you survive
That piece will always be a part of you

But, even then, happiness is still the key
It's the only thing that matters afterwards
It may have changed me
But I mastered it and beat it
Because I am strong, even if it took a bit

Eyden Gonzalez
8th Grade
Sharyland North High School
Mission, TX

OVERCOME

Society is filled with battles
Battles that are
That are testing us with
With hard obstacles

Hard obstacles that we got
We got to confront
Confront with all our might
All our might that make us
That make us stronger

Stronger than ever
Than ever before
Before it made you

Made you into a fearless
A fearless person who is
Who is not afraid
Not afraid to face
Face the life obstacles

Life obstacles that are still
Are still testing us
Testing us with challenges
Challenges that we will
We will overcome throughout
Throughout our bravery

Bravery that gives us
Give us more strength
Strength that boosts
Boosts our confidence

Confidence that makes us
Makes us into a warrior
A warrior who has been
Who has been through a lot of

A lot of battles
Battles that got shattered
Shattered into pieces

Sujeis Perez
12th Grade
Sharyland Pioneer High School
Mission, TX

OUR ART OF REBIRTH

Our rebirth,
The opportunity to see ourselves once more,
To feel,
To see,
To know,
Even heal.

My rebirth,
The opportunity to miss our beloved,
To feel our loss,
To see their graves,
To know we're alone,
Maybe be able to heal.

Our rebirth,
The opportunity to be able to change our choices,
To feel new,
To see a better change,
To know we're capable,
Maybe even heal.

Our rebirth,
The opportunity to be more than just amiable,
To feel reborn,
To see ambitious dreams come to life,
To know we're courageous and diligent,
Manage to heal.

Our rebirth,
Is more than just an opportunity,
More than just a feeling,
More than a simple change,
More than even we would expect to know, understand,
More than health.

Our rebirth,
Is a miraculous return,
A hope for a better us,

Is a gift from my God,
A little proof that shows I'm capable of something better,
Absolute health.

Our rebirth is a new beginning,
Is a moment you appreciate and resolve,
Your past doings,
However, it all begins with
Our rebirth.

Vanessa Vega
12th Grade
Sharyland High School

About the Editors

Edward Vidaurre's poems have appeared in The New York Times Magazine, The Texas Observer, Avalon Literary Review, The Acentos Review, Poetrybay, Voices de la Luna, as well as other journals and anthologies. Vidaurre is the author of six collections of poetry with his seventh forthcoming in March 2020. He is the 2018-2019 City of McAllen, TX Poet Laureate, a two time Pushcart Prize nominated poet and publisher of FlowerSong Books, Vidaurre is from Boyle Heights, CA and now resides in McAllen, TX with his wife and daughter.

Rodney Gomez is the author of *Citizens of the Mausoleum*, a finalist for the John A. Robertson Award from the Texas Institute of Letters. His other poetry collections include *Ceremony of Sand* and the forthcoming *Arsenal* with Praise Song and Geographic Tongue, winner of the Pleiades Press Visual Poetry Series. He will serve as the 2020- 2021 McAllen Poet Laureate. He lives in McAllen, Texas with his family.

Priscilla Celina Suarez was the 2015-2017 McAllen Poet Laureate. Lina is co-author of the Texas State Library's Bilingual Programs chapter, co-founder of the Gloria Anzaldua Legacy Project, and member of the Chocholichex Writing Collective. She is the author of the YA book *Cuentos Wela Told Me: That Scared the Beeswax Out of Me!*. Her work appears in such venues *as ¡Juventud!: Growing up on the Border* and *Along the River III: Dark Voices from the Río Grande*.

www.ingramcontent.com/pod-product-compliance
Lightning Source LLC
Chambersburg PA
CBHW071144090426
42736CB00012B/2223